# Jet-Powered Funny Cars

Jesse Young

**Reading consultant:**

John Manning, Professor of Reading

University of Minnesota

Capstone Press

MINNEAPOLIS

Printed in the United States of America.

Capstone Press • 2440 Fernbrook Lane • Minneapolis, MN 55447

Editorial Director    John Coughlan
Managing Editor    John Martin
Copy Editor    Gil Chandler

*Library of Congress Cataloging-in-Publication Data*

Young, Jesse, 1941-
  Jet-powered funny cars / by Jesse Young.
      p. cm.-- (Cruisin')
  Includes bibliographical references and index.
  ISBN 1-56065-220-9
  1. Funny cars--Juvenile literature.  [1. Drag racing.
2. Automobiles, Racing.]  I. Title.  II. Series.
TL236.23.Y68   1995
629.228--dc20                                        94-26774
                                                          CIP
                                                          AC
ISBN: 1-56065-220-9

99 98 97 96 95             8 7 6 5 4 3 2 1

# Table of Contents

# *Chapter 1*

# **Jet Cars at the Track**

Two jet-powered funny cars pull up to the starting line. The pole of lights set between the cars flashes yellow. The drivers wait for the green light to signal the start of the race.

At Raceway Park, in Englishtown, New Jersey, jet-car stars Lynn Redeman and his opponent are about to light up the sky. They power up the jet-propelled red-and-blue **exhausts** to dazzle the fans. Then they blow down the quarter-mile (402.3-meter) drag strip in five seconds flat.

If you were standing closer than 200 feet (about 60 meters) behind their powerful funny

cars, the heat of the engines would have burned the hair off your arms.

They may look something like ordinary cars, but jet-powered funny cars run on **nitromethane**, a jet-rocket fuel. They are drag-racing cars with fiberglass bodies and front-mounted engines.

Jet-powered funny cars do not race for prize money. Instead, drivers and crews work to set new speed records. The cars appear on the race circuit as an exhibition only.

It's an exhibition that few fans ever forget.

**The huge engine makes the driver look small in this jet-powered dragster.**

9

# *Chapter 2*

# **The First Jet Cars**

W alter Arfons is an important part of the jet-car story. An amateur mechanic, he built the first jet cars in 1960 and tried them out on the Bonneville Salt Flats in Utah.

Several others started building them soon after. In 1963, Craig Breedlove set a record speed of 407.4 miles (656.1 kilometers) per hour in a jet car called *Spirit of America*. Breedlove's jet-powered car had three wheels and looked more like an airplane than a car.

A year later, Walter Arfons' jet car, the *Wingfoot Express*, was driven by Tom Green. Green broke Breedlove's record with a speed

**A drag parachute slows driver Roger Gustin and his jet-powered car.**

of 413.2 miles (665.4 kilometers) per hour.
Walt's brother, Art, then beat that record in his
*Green Monster* at 434.0 miles (698.9
kilometers) per hour.

Arfons and other mechanics built many of
these early jet-powered cars with engines from
military aircraft. The engines came from
fighter planes used in the Korean War (1950-
1953). In the 1960s **surplus** engines that had

originally cost more than half a million dollars each were being sold for as little as $3,000. The engines were made of steel and **titanium**. The cars weighed from 2,500 to 3,500 pounds (933 to 1306 kilograms).

These cars were dangerous. And there were no rules for racing them. Breedlove and Arfons risked their lives in their heavy jet-engine cars. At high speeds, the two parachutes that open to slow down a car would sometimes tear away. The **brake linings** of the cars often burned out.

Many people said that jet-powered cars should not take part in land-speed competition. They argued that only **piston-engine** cars should be allowed to compete.

In 1962, the National Hot Rod Association banned jet-powered cars from racing on any of its **circuits**. That **ban** lasted until 1974, when Roger Gustin came along.

# *Chapter 3*

# **Roger Gustin**

Roger Gustin knows the business of jet cars better than anyone else. When Gustin graduated from high school in 1957, he dreamed of becoming a professional race-car driver.

He got his start at Raven Rock Dragstrip, in Portsmouth, Ohio, where he raced his 1949 Chevrolet **hot rod**. Roger kept his dream alive while working a factory job by day and working on his car at night. With no tools, shop, or crew behind him, he had only his determination.

Roger bought a 1955 Chevrolet with a **V-8** engine, and asked his brother Phil to help him

**Roger Gustin leans against the chassis of his jet-powered funny car.**

as the team mechanic. Together the Gustin brothers raced well and moved up the ranks in **Sportsman** (**amateur**) classes. By 1965 they were ready for professional racing.

## The Business of Racing

Roger still needed to raise money and learn the business of racing. This meant more than

**The driver is protected by a strong helmet and a roll bar. In case of a crash, he'll need them.**

learning bookkeeping. Roger studied public relations, advertising, and marketing. He went to acting school to learn how to make television commercials for his **sponsors**.

Roger Gustin's cars have carried the names of many sponsors: Smith Brothers' cough drops, Valvoline oil, Lava soap, and Black &

**Jolly Rancher and Castrol are two companies that sponsor this jet-powered funny car.**

Decker tools.  These companies help Roger pay for his cars, equipment, and crew.

Roger created the *Lava Machine* with Procter & Gamble in 1987.  That year the Gustin-Lava team reached a speed of 275 miles (442.8 kilometers) per hour and won all 40 races on the circuit.  It was a record that put Roger in the *Guinness Book of World Records*. He was interviewed on television more than

1,000 times.  Over 50 magazines ran stories about him.

In 1972, Roger made an important decision. He gave up hot rods for the most dangerous cars in motor sports–jet cars.

## New Jet Cars

Roger wanted to build a new kind of jet car that was lightweight and safe.  He immediately started talking with the National Hot Rod Association (NHRA).  He tried to persuade this important organization to license jet cars.

The NHRA did this in November, 1974, and Roger became the first driver to be licensed to race a jet car.  Just two weeks later, Roger Gustin was named to the National Hot Rod Association Hall of Fame.

## Replica Jet Cars

In 1980, Gustin built the first jet-powered car in a fiberglass **replica** of a regular car body. This new car looked like a regular car and not like an airplane.

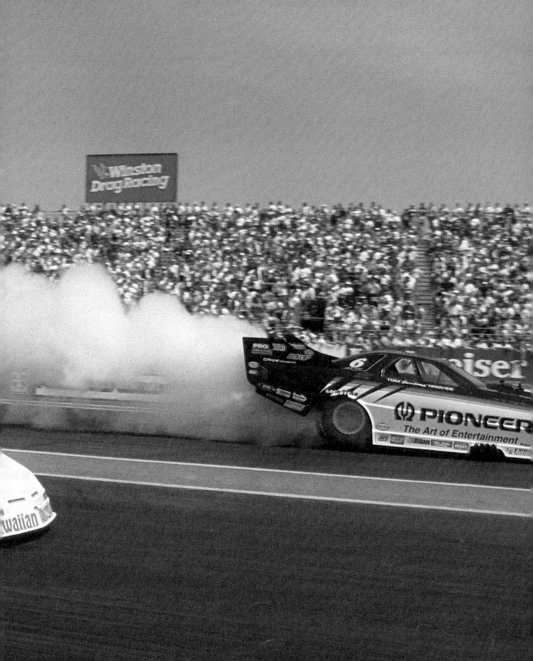

When Roger Gustin started building jet cars, there were only about seven or eight around. Today there are more than 70 jet cars.

The Gustin cars have won more races and set more records than any of these other jet cars. Gustin now has two racing teams. Both are sponsored by Workmat Corporation. One team races a 1992 Chevrolet Beretta, and the other a 1994 Chevrolet Lumina. Each is powered by a **Pratt and Whitney JT-12** jet engine. With spare parts added and wages paid, the two teams cost Gustin about $500,000 a year.

Each of his cars *looks* like a street-model Chevrolet. Up close, however, you can see that the **aerodynamic** bodies are made of **carbon fiber**, a lightweight material. His Firestone tires are mounted on aluminum wheels and fitted for performance, safety, and appearance.

## In the Shop

Roger's jet-car business, in Franklin Furnace, Ohio, lies just a few miles from the family farm where he grew up. His team maintains a large shop. The shop has every spare part and tool necessary to keep these high-tech cars running. Next to the shop sit the semi-tractor-trailer **tow rigs** that carry the cars to 40 racing events every year.

In 1992, Roger spent the year recovering from leg injuries after a near-fatal crash. When he returned to the funny-car circuit, he decided to give up racing to try something new. He became director of AutoStar Productions. This company sponsors 22 events every year. Together these events are called the Super Chevrolet Show.

**Roger Gustin's *Lava Machine***

# *Chapter 4*

# **Afterburners**

When asked why he owns and drives jet-powered funny cars, Roger Gustin says: "Driving a race car equipped with an **afterburner** is the most exciting thing there is."

You will not find afterburners on any piston-engine cars, or even on commercial airplanes. You find them only on military aircraft and on jet-powered funny cars.

An afterburner is an **auxiliary**, or extra, engine attached to the rear of the regular jet engine. It burns the unused gas-air mixture from the **exhaust**. This extra burning more

**The auxiliary engines are attached at the rear of the regular jet engine.**

than doubles the engine's power. The driver feels this extra power in the constant acceleration of the car, as measured by **g-force**. Once you light an afterburner, it never lets up.

### The G-force

G-force stands for gravitational force. Most cars, even Top Fuel dragsters, accelerate and then reach a top speed. In a regular car, you accelerate to 1.2 g-force and then settle down to about 1 g-force.

A jet-powered funny car actually accelerates to 4.8 g-force—almost five times the pull of the earth's gravity. This means that when the driver accelerates, he feels a force on him that is 4.8 times his own body weight. When he shuts the engine off, the driver's weight is 7 times less than his usual body weight. If he were not harnessed, his body would fly right out of his seat.

That is how the afterburner acceleration *feels*. But how does it work?

## The Extra Thrust

In the jet-engine's afterburner, fresh fuel is sprayed into the exhaust, where the gas-air mixture causes the fuel to **ignite**. The increased combustion causes the exhaust to expand, even more than in standard jet engines. That is how additional thrust is created.

The body lifts up on *Sonic Thunder II* to expose the chassis, cockpit, and jet engine.

Whenever the afterburner is used, the thrust doubles. A funny car using nitromethane fuel creates 3,000 pounds (1,119.7 kilograms) of thrust. With an afterburner added, the car blows out 6,000 pounds (2,239.4 kilograms) of thrust.

Afterburners use more fuel than regular jet engines and are used only for short periods. On military aircraft, the afterburner allows a quick escape after dropping a bomb. Bombers and fighters also use the afterburner while taking off from the dangerously short deck of an aircraft carrier. In both cases, the use of the afterburner lasts only about ten seconds.

Drag races are only a quarter of a mile (402.3 meters) long. The **elapsed time** is usually around five seconds. The afterburner operates the whole time.

# *Chapter 5*

# **Look and Performance**

You can get a close-up look at what a jet-powered funny car looks, smells, and sounds like at any of the National Hot Rod Association tracks. For an extra charge, you can sometimes go right into the pits and watch the crews work on their cars.

## Safety

You will probably see many Chevrolet models that have been transformed into jet cars. Most of the bodies are made of a lightweight carbon-fiber material.

TIM RICHARDS

SUPERWINCH

They have at least one escape hatch when the car body is locked down. This escape is usually through the roof or a removable windshield. The hatch can be released easily from either inside or outside the car.

The driver's compartment is made of aluminum or steel. There is only one seat. No passengers are allowed in funny cars during a race.

In addition, the driver is held in the seat by a heavy-duty seatbelt system. The belts have to be replaced every two years.

The driver is protected from the **intake** and **compressor**–where the air is taken into the engine–by an aluminum shield about one-half inch (2.5 centimeters) thick.

All funny cars have a fire extinguisher on board. The driver's suit is completely fireproof, and so are the driver's gloves, boots, and helmet.

At least two parachutes are part of the control system of a jet-powered funny car. The primary chute shuts off the engine when it is released at the end of a race. The secondary chute is operated separately in case something happens to the primary one.

## Performance Limits

The National Hot Rod Association sets limits on how fast jet cars can go. The jet funny car is allowed 290 miles (467 kilometers) per hour. The highest speed on record is 285 miles (458.9 kilometers) per hour in a licensed jet car. If funny cars exceed these limits, their drivers receive heavy fines. For one to ten miles (1.6 to 16 kilometers) per hour over the limit, the fine is $500 on a first offense. For the third offense, the fine for each mile over the limit is $5,000.

## The Future

Sixty million fans come to see jet-powered funny cars every year. What does the future hold for jet-powered funny cars?

Roger Gustin was one of the racers to make the first exhibition trip to Japan in 1989. It was a big success. People are now crowding the racetracks to see jet-powered funny cars in the United States, Japan, Europe, New Zealand, and Australia. The future of the jet-powered funny car is growing brighter all the time.

# Glossary

**aerodynamic**–a shape designed to cut smoothly through air resistance

**afterburner**–an extra engine attached to a regular jet engine in which fresh fuel is sprayed into the exhaust, causing it to ignite and to create more combustion

**amateur**–someone who is not a professional

**auxiliary**–something additional that aids or supports

**ban**–to make something illegal or against the rules

**brake linings**–the surface of a brake that contacts the brake pads

**carbon fiber**–an extremely strong, lightweight material, mixed with resin similar to fiberglass

**circuit**–teams, clubs, or arenas that form an association for competition

**compression**–the process of putting air under pressure

**elapsed time**–the time it takes to get from the starting line to the finish line

**exhaust**–the burned fuel-air mixture that produces thrust in a jet engine

**g-force**–the unit of force exerted on a still object by the pull of gravity

**hot rod**–a production car that has been modified to go faster

**ignite**–to set fire to

**intake**–the opening in the front of a jet engine where air is drawn in

**nitromethane**–a special kind of rocket fuel used in funny cars and Top Fuelers

**piston engine**–an engine with parts (or pistons) that move up and down inside the engine's cylinders

**Pratt & Whitney JT-12**–the name and model number of a jet engine

**replica**–a copy of something

**sponsor**–a company which gives a racing team money in exchange for advertising on the cars

**Sportsman class**–the beginning competitive racing class

**surplus**–having more than is needed

**titanium**–a strong, metal part used in aircraft metals to give stability at high temperatures

**tow rigs**–chains or cables for pulling cars

**V-8**–an engine with eight pistons arranged in a "V" formation of four pistons per side

# To Learn More

Barrett, Norman. *Dragsters.* New York: Franklin Watts, 1987.

Connolly, Maureen. *Dragsters.* Mankato, MN: Capstone Press, 1992.

Creighton, Susan. *Funny Cars.* Mankato, MN: Crestwood House, 1988.

Edmonds, I.G. *Funny Car Racing for Beginners.* New York: Rinehart and Winston, 1982.

Estrem, Paul. *Rocket-Powered Cars.* Mankato, MN: Crestwood House, 1987.

# Some Useful Addresses

**ProJet Association**
P.O. Box 325
Etna, OH 43018

**National Hot Rod Association (NHRA)**
2035 Financial Way
Glendora, CA 91740

**International Hot Rod Association**
P.O. Box 3029
Bristol, TN 37625

# Acknowledgments

Special thanks to Roger Gustin and ProJet for background and historical information; to the National Hot Rod Association for safety and technical guidelines; and to Dan Cunningham, Technical Advisor.

# Index

*Photo Credits:*

National Hot Rod Association: pp. 4, 14, 20, 22-23, 34,
36-37; Roger Gustin: pp. 12, 13, 16, 40; Leslie Lovett: pp.
6-7, 8,10, 17, 18, 19, 26, 28, 29, 30, 32.